barefoot
in the temple

Selected

Poetry

Of

R.T. Romero

Copyright © 2016 Richard T. Romero

ISBN: 978-0-9898689-2-1

Onyx

Our lives touch in tongues
        in ways spun and woven
Twin flames of art
        and reason are spoken
Enchained act of freedom
        weak links it has none:
Unburdening seasons
        like deer leap and run...
Thrill this awakened heart
        dancing being of light
Enveloping, opening oceanic sight...
        intently scry thy inner eye,
Compressing time, intensify,
pour molten meaning
        into my conversation:
Our lives touch and part
affecting far paths
        and choices, glancing
Unto the moment,
        and returned alert:
        trembling at thy doorstep
            openly sublime
            to thee I bow.

Alone I enter
Alone I leave
For me alone my own will grieve
And I will lie unknowing
        though my deeds will carry on:
        ripples on the night wind
        carrying my song
What child of light has seen the night?
What night has known full day?
If I should use a master's voice
        his servant do I stay.

Cusp

Holding to the center

The eternal rose in the circling garden
Shines like a star of living radiance:
Within this cusp I see you
Smiling in still water.

White pebbles form the pathway
Beneath the graceful arch:
There your hand caressed
This fragrant petal.

Because the wineglass rests
It is not empty.

Same

Like hovering flames in the wind of the night
Hoping on hope that the wishing is right
The captives of time in this life mystery
To soar or to grovel, in debt or free
Where all in each moment is both lost and gained
And each of all lovers is pleasured and pained
Where servant and master are humbled and praised
And the dreams of the nations are lowered and
raised...
What constant is present when all else is gone
When even the stars are the heralds of dawn?

Paths

The lady seems to always know
The secret paths that make dreams grow:
Toward the light that satiates
Awareness gently gravitates.

Though swayed by winds that waft unseen
Her sensual dance has always been:
Since time began for humankind,
Desire has moved the heart and mind.

Her body holds a slumbering fire
That from a man must draw desire:
The hunter drawn by her enchantment
Finds himself on his knees rampant.

An old man walking by the sea
Related all of this to me:
Whoever would behold true glory
Let them craft of life their story.

Luck

Life runs like the tumbling dice
We wager with each throw:
Searching through the fire and ice
Without the means to know.
In answer to our questing dream
Inspiring ardor's goal and stream
Forever evolving each and other
Falter not, my younger brother:
Without the courage to carry on
There is no quest, nor hope of dawn.
Faded in a shadowed veil
The old man has his tales to tell:
The journey of humanity
Is very much the same to me.
Beyond the grave, and out of date
In my heart I still relate.
Time beyond
And now time still
Knowing how we really feel
Life and breath in every heart
Timeless, ageless, works of art
In this life are those who care:
Between them bonds a common share...
Are hearts so odd at soulful root
When moved to mourn the bitter fruit?
When winging wild in twilit skies
Or singing songs and lullabies
Or kindling up the freedom flame
What difference find, save flesh and name?
If naught is common in the bond
That poets share, in soul beyond
The reach of weak mortality,
Then where is Man's nobility?

Tender 2

My darling's eyes
Are distant with pain
Despite which she smiles:
Sunlight on Rain.
Her smiles haunt me as echoing dreams
Eyes a-sparkle, rapt, it seems
A soul in a cusp of mystery
Sipping a twin to history:
Spiritual presences, present always
Echoing steps in wooden hallways...
In the night, all too alone,
   Utterly vast where starlight shone
    a whorl of worlds
sworn and swirled
  pinwheeling in godsbreath, reeling...
   What is my task? Why am I sent?
Which gods watch her, that I am spent?
Insightful endurance
     Beneath her awareness
        As she converses
           With clinical glance
Her heartful of whim
    She adroitly reverses
        And, wonderous, shyly asks me to
dance.
Such a magnificent soul
    fine as pearls on black silk
       incisive as a Toledo blade
       loving as mother's milk
Sweet bringings of happiness, boon to her aid
      as if of one we two were made...
       and she thinks to ask:
        Why is it?

Vixen

The vixen pauses on upthrust stone
 Panting, hot, almost alone
Below, in the crystal pool so clean,
 Reflecting the ring where tall trees lean,
The quenching water awaits her tongue
 As her ears search about for her playful young.
Above the forest the hawk careens
 The winds arise, and the tall tree keens:
You ARE beautiful, daughter,
 May every happiness fill your heart.

rhyme

A million temptations
    a handful of rhyme
Scatter the ashes
    and break out the wine...

Broth

My campfire warms my calloused hands
In misting morn in Irish lands
And honing up my well-worn blade
I see a warrior lass well made.

In silence as my wont to be
I note the heavy heart of she
And reaching for my battered cup
I fill with broth for her to sup.

And noting in her eye a tear
Where shines a pride that conquers fear
I give her my embattled smile
And bid her welcome here awhile.

Wing

Potent femme, of poise and balance,
          I sometimes speak awry,
but when, enrapt, you bond my glance
          my motives clarify.

I pace you for a further mood
          engaging every step
deep into your darkness woo'd
          to see a secret kept.

And when across the vasting gulf
          I seek to catch your eye
My thoughts arrayed are not enough
          Until they to you fly.

Lion

Like an aging Lion
The importance of my pride
Grows in direct proportion
To the absence at my side.

No true companion to share a good meal,
No welcoming smiles, to make my home real
No conversation to make my thoughts bright
No way to know if what's wrong is alright.

Cold swirls of logic wash sandy wet stone
Where I am left breathing with soulheart alone
To gaze back upon the well-meaning dance
And quietly mourn the loss of a chance.

Like the swift bird
        She flew.

Carol

A sphere of light
Within the dark
Where mingling hearts
Have caught a spark
Outweighing all reality
And promised immortality.

The sweep of time gathers up my chords
And scatters dreams among her wards
Each chime a bell of found relation;
Each a crown of new elation.

Her hands pluck tones from out of air
New thoughts stir us up to care
Blending in melodious tunes
To strike upon the breast like runes:

What night is this beneath the star
That sleeping we see who we are?

Athens

Legacy of three thousand years
This pillar in the breeze
Beneath the same bright brassy sky
Above the Ionian Sea
A slave boy sat and polished stone
And whistled all the while
Not knowing that his work would stand
When the palace was a pile:
What is worth the doing then?
What stands when all is ruined?
Its just the heart of a whistling lad
Though I don't recall the tune...

Healer

The well is in your heart
And the pool there is clean:
Drawing up from within,
    the act is refreshing.
Close the door on all the world
For a moment of calm knowing
Feel the seeds within your dream
Within your own life growing...
        Honor your innocent desire
Focus on aspiration's fire
Uphold the consequence of details within:
                To know is not a sin.
       The world is in your grasp, and fair,
       You are here for a good reason
       Just move the puzzle with care:
       And success is in your season.
  Target the target
Aim not too low
    What you can believe in
Is where you can go.

Poets

Like walking shadows about a dark place
The nomads worship their passion's face
To seek an amusement that flickers away
So petulant it can last but a day

Though seldom arising to evoke the new,
Directing their eyes to avoid a bright view
Scorning the compasses guiding the few:
Scorning Polaris, who's guiding our sails,
Scorning the Moon, and scorning the tales
Telling of journeys of heroes and scouts
Preferring to scribble their dabbling pouts.

A poet creates to inspire the passions,
Regardless of boredom,
Regardless of fashions;
Arising from ruins and braving the flames,
Grimly determined to write the gods' names,
At last striding free from their heart's devastation
And urging the brave to establish a nation.

Ruby

        I stand in check,
At the threshold of your world, trembling,
Arrayed in a thousand manifested dreams
Enmeshing sensations into our now
I step
Into solid, of dreamlight,
Bare warm foot to cool marble:
Moonlight and stars sharpen my hunger
Sensing beyond, from the garden, a fragrance of
dew:
        Integral core to furthest vision
Defying probability and reason
           A divine madness surely
           Is this love, unsought,
unbidden, inevitable...
Through this door
        to begin
separating cause from effect
moment from eternal silence
           crushing doubt with decision
To hold you
To cherish you
To be, in a kiss:
        Like shadows thrown by firelight
        I awaken, rising to your scent
           Clean as water.
Lips to a rosebud: so we touch, tentative,
Sensing skin silk to silk, heart to beating heart,
A strong hand to lift you, full and ripe,
        Driven hearts pulsing ever ahead
The racing horses in their own wind...
        to pause in a sip, eyes over rim:
        I know the crystal loves the wine,
           and savor your mouth.

Vine

When all the world has been and seen
These tokens of our mortal dream
And young men age who've never been
                  Creators, yet unspoken,
Then climb the mountain and tell all
In heavens reach, from where stars fall
Within the sphere that now defines
The secret depths and hidden signs
'til wondering dawn rises to view,
And spreads her glow on questions true,
Which, brought to light, can evoke change
Though not quite all within our range:
           Overlooked, the details show it...
Then go you home to carry on
Before the light is wholly gone
To sing aloud the last refrain
And write your verse upon the rain
To reach and grasp and write their hearts
As if a demigod of arts
To plow and plant the yet unseeing
Upon their very ground of being:
           Planting there, would you grow it?
However sure and deft your hand
Respond to what is never planned.
Far down the echoed way ahead
Where others write and we're long dead
So far beyond this mortal frame,
So far beyond this clever game,
Please speak mine only in my name
           Though of your heart I stole it.
Hearken now and scurry fast
The vineyard's son is home at last!
           What alchemy transmutes the line
From new crushed grape to finest wine?

Dirge

Sunrise east and sunset west
Cross my hands upon my breast
Now has fled my dying breath
My footfalls touch the halls of death.
Where now wanders our sweet love
Forgotten by the gods above?
Tears are fallen in the dust
And yet you go, as the living must.
At the sounding of the bell
Solemnly at evening knell
Take this rose from my hand fell
Find happiness, and fare thee well:
Know thee love has conquered all
Hearts forever in sad thrall
Hearts forever in sad thrall
Find Happiness, and love thee well.

Eagles

Solitude walks out
onto the plain
alone in the silence
and wet with the rain
each striding bravely
to try it once more
the sourcing of happiness
inside love's door.
If we, as two eagles,
are soaring to pair,
well met in our balance
and harmony fair,
the world seems to pause
for the rythmning rhyme
and opens up pathways
which leap space and time.

We will kiss in sheets of lightning
And touch in rolling thunder.

Hope

To touch, to grasp her tender flame
To write with starlight just her name
To reach and hold in empty air
Though all alone I sense her there
Is summoning my primal heat
A storm of surging heart abeat
Once more a phoenix in new life
In hope, and dream, with passions rife
With calling voice like home to yearn
A world within from which to learn,
With wisdoms many lifetimes old
And laughter pure as molten gold
Like dreaming bells within a trance
All haunting, like a lover's dance,
Caressing now this poet's heart
And writes thereon, with finer art.

Daisies

Happiness, like a beckoning dawn
Whispers soft a tender song
Unfolding within you and me
To grow from dream: reality.
Like daisies nodding by our path
Fresh with dew in sunlight's bath
Sentiments awake may stir
As hands we clasp, and hearts concur.
How I yearn for you, tonight
My love, though out of sight,
But as I long to hold you near
I shall await your beckon here.

Oak

To gaze upon a further star
To thrust my consciousness so far
To hold aloft that lamp anew
And know her warmth in mind and thew
Is here to me, this hour to bring
A new born song for hearts to sing
As old as our own kind has been
And yet a seed, the Oak within.

Starlight

A life of moment entering
Amid the songs the angels sing
At edge of hearing, on spirit winds,
As mortal loves transcend the sins
Aware as skin upon the thorn
Thus roses kiss, of heaven born.

Unsought faults must fall to naught,
With lessons learned and learning taught,
Without foreknowledge, without intent,
Unplanned, simple, and elegant,
And all within these souls we see
Each so pure, in reality.

Walk

You move the way I'd love to write
And wear your skin as warm as light
Your feet are precious in their poise
And hands so sweet with crafted joys
Your hair bears scents of sandalwood
Your voice speaks wisdoms deep and good
Your face inspires this dreaming son
Above those curves of desires won
Your eyes, like frostfire in the night...
Oh woman, you were my delight!

Light

O radiant waves of photons bright
Graduated sphere of light
Warming all mortality
Of the earth as of the sea
Within this eye and in my heart
Granting power to my art
Feed my spirit, air, and earth,
Water, wood, and stone of birth
Life in all fecundity
Known orb of all reality
Nurture love within our hearts
And let our living thrill our arts.

Source

From deep, deep down within your soil
Beneath your darkest mines of toil
The source of strength seeps out to fill
The singing one who haunts you still.

This power fills to brim the cup
Which poets sip, to conjure up
Awakenings within your night
Of druid's art and minstrel's light.

Within your spirit feel it grow
Infusing substance where you go
The source of dancing laughs aloud
And of the common breeds the proud.

Rose Petal Soul

So tender is this
to a Rose petal soul:
A heart-sourced kiss
Within each, a whole.
Caresses like balm
In caring, and calm:
Inspire old wounds to newly heal
Where ancient promises youthfully seal.
And in the glow of our new dawn
And all our wisdoms unite as one
Magnificent heartfires sear and bind
Meeting, mating, mind to mind
Nightwind sparks, from aching dreams,
Grow wild free passions to bond the seams...
And after all, in beloved view,
And heart beats quote the songs sung true:
When satisfaction quietly mends,
O spirit friend, whom heaven sends,
My eyes will shine in love for you
My lips in silence will speak true
To reach once more, awaking,
To find your smile within my taking
I shine with heat, my metal glows:
Your forge is hard, my hammer knows
You temper me: this blade you whet
You balance me, eternally met:
Show me to your dragon's heart
To slay that fear with strength and art.

Shadow Raven

birdbone whistles, leather drums,
and chantings pause when Raven comes
eyes alert and dark with craft
watching close in history's draft

running strong in mistaken course
tripping alarms toward dread remorse...
like starving wolves they circled aware,
canceling each other's craft and flair,
till wide of the mark speculations wound
and for all that promise, lost holy ground.
Now, where might have grown a nation
fruitful flowering souls in elation
gather the mourning winds of loss
where love lies wounded on friendship's moss.

birdbone whistles, leather drums,
and chantings pause where Raven comes,
ever wise with craft flies he
gifting a hope where none should be.

found thy nation
on communication

Present

After fading light returns,
        And shadows draw away,
Discovered meaning sometimes earns
        New light for the day.

Align intentions toward the good
        Scattered from intent
The acorn sprouts from seed to wood
        So History breeds content.

Awareness of the stories told
        When we by campfires mused
Foretells to us how lives unfold
        And how they should be used.

The tales describe our course and weighs
        The values we steer by
And darkling waters swirling deep
        Provoke our questions 'Why'.

So not alone is history read
        Nor is its thrust unbound
But by our heart and wondering head
        Our present life is found.

Bowl

Blue jade bowl
       and flowered hand
Holds warm my life
       in this icy land.
This heart of sacred living light
       was trusting as an arrow's flight
A flight which swept away my strength
       with no time left for time at length.
That time is gone, and yet I stay
       the passing into night of day,
I hold my candle in the wind
       and cup this light against that end
Against the dark of my feared doom
       denying what I might assume
And wait amid the silent songs
       that sing of where my heart belongs
Accepting all whom you must be
       Awaiting dawning eyes to see
Again perhaps you'll call me near
       when I approach in braver fear
A fear that light might once again
       be drowned within that haunted fen.

Dancer

She is dancing through the air
And all alone I meet her there
From my reach she moves away,
And dancing, smiles as bright as day
Yet in the still night's forest pool
Among deep trees with waters cool
Reflecting stars and sipping deer
She comes in dreams to draw me near...

Within my shelter build my craft
With fire and wood and windy draft
With crystals and the river stone
Building magic, word and tone,
I pause in song to see you fly
And smile a friendly lullabye.

Iris

In stillness close your eyes with me
And reach for deep eternity
Drawing light within the dark
Until your essence catches spark
Unfolding like the forest moon
A life refreshed a dream in tune.
Within the dance of deepest dreams
Where the iris blooms and moonlight gleams
The heartfires light and share the heat
And dancers weave on nimble feet
I dance with you, and know the glow
Of ageless light which hearts bestow
This cup I offer sweet with spice
Is it a dream without a price?
Mere fantasy, a spinning word,
Hardly a seed, or egg of bird,
Cradled in a moonlit nest
Just like this heart within my chest.
I cup your iris to my lips
And draw on life in gentle sips
To nibble at the bloom of life
And in your eyes I find my...

Feral

How can I tame this ravenous heart?
Where passions, like wolves, howl feral art?
While poems and songs may mingle pure,
Foundations shake with what I endure.

Internal lightning strikes wild in my night
Stone crags crumble, and trees catch light,
Change, like winds in crescendos of doom,
All in the quiet of a hermit's room.

I seethe again with a passion's fire
Fighting for life, to love I aspire,
Risking it all on a throw of the dice
And watch as the rest, in fire or ice.

Though this chance already seems totally lost
Again cast aside at high personal cost,
Yet must I hold on, my angels beside,
Til I fall exhausted, at the end of the ride....

How did I come by this stony-eyed gaze?
This granitic facade when worlds within blaze?
Had I shown her the storms that rage wild in my
veins
Then love would have feared, and might never
reign.

Cat

She dances with a feline strength
That makes me shy, although at length
And bolder might have joined her dance
And caught her mood, perhaps her glance,
Yet there alone her moves are pure
And now I loneliness endure.
Her eyes so blue and clear with sight
With all the magic of the night
Ensorcelling the boy in me
So helpless, till she set me free...
Her mouth so quick with living smiles
Disarms my wit and foils my wiles
So strong and pure she apprehends
My clumsy effort, which offends,
Yet with a gentle smile for me
Opens her hand and sets me free...

Reprise

A dance within a secret place
Where spirits reach to touch a face
Of divinity, sharing incandescent,
A human act, yet luminescent.

Rapt souls savor, lingering
Embracing passions, mingling,
Sweeping onward into flight
With trust, like godlings, to requite
Empowered with immortal scores
Empathic harmony, which soars
Balanced as the stars tonight
Guided by internal light.

And so I stand on darkling's plain,
Alone in darkness, wet with rain...

Wish

When I wish upon the star
I try to venture who we are
That now within eternity
We become who we could be.

Is it such a phantom hope
Is not the end within our scope
That even in mortality
We grow beyond futility?

Concurrent with a phasing moon
Within the shifting future, soon
Is marked a blaze of destiny
Defining new reality.

Prophet

Not so strange, or stranger too,
That within this danger visions true
And unbeknownst a heart might rise
To beckon night with lullabyes
And as on wings launch out in air
Full knowing there is hope bourne there.

I've walked afar this devastation
Being bred to know this nation
So bright with her beckoning aires
In the warm hovels as in the faires
Wherever hearts and hands may merge
Wherever passions storm and surge

But all alight the glowing face
Of one bright child of Adam's race
Who singles out the question true
Would you be and know value?
Would you see the heart of she
Who met the prophet at the sea?

The gods have brought us now to this:
Is there meaning in a poet's kiss?

Web

With fiery minds we created a world
Where dreams conspired and labors hurled
Into a thread of electric night
To gaze and craft with new insight
To meet and touch each other's mind
To laugh and love, and eventually find
New consciousness emerging clear,
As far from sleep as a mystic seer.

Indigo

Jewel of my desert,
       arising in the East,
Set in indigo everness,
       bright eyed serenity's feast.

Drawn the eye must find you,
       splendid and alone,
To pierce the dark forever,
       revealing the unknown.

My heart would cast a wishing,
       a sourcing there in you,
To shine with such a brilliance,
       eternal, pure, and true.

Yet mortal is the framework,
       the path has led us on,
Your startling spell diminished,
       within approaching dawn.

Anxious in rebirth
       I search the broadest earth...

Aspire

Woven with reality
The context meets the dream
Balancing duality
Where ancient fissures steam
Beneath the crags of seeing
Above my passion's fire
Within a sky of being
Releasing my desire.

A moment comes of wellness
As if to hold the moon
Resounding within silence
The stillness I attune...

Morning

Awaiting the morning
        in the cold of false dawn
While star fields pass slowly
        and the night lingers on
Awake in each minute
        in the season of Spring
Awake for the morning
        when the meadowlarks sing.
I wait in the forest
        where the leaves grow anew
All wet in the starlight
        with the freshness of dew
I wait on the mountain
        where the light first will shine
I wait for the morning
        When my love will be mine.

Annie Mordell

Stepping from shadows,
          her ghostspirit talks
Opening old doors
          where had been only locks
Enabling vistas
          where had been only dreams
Pointing toward knowledge
          where humanity gleams
Oh, Annie, where are you tonight?
Twenty years gone,
          yet I read by your light.

Whisper

It takes two hearts to mingle
        Two hearts free
Two people knowing
        To make a love be.

I gaze in a dreaming
        Upon a tall tree
Noticing daylight
        Recalls you to me.

I walk to the Oak
        From an acorn has grown
And ask him if my love
        Might ever be known.

The Oak stands a moment
        Then creaks a slow smile
And answers in whispers
        that mean "Wait awhile..."

Solitude

To be in silent solitude
        As open to the world
As on a mountain, gazing
        With pennant proud unfurled,
To grasp the being, firmly,
        Without distraction's feint
And know the meaning of the soul
        And that for which I'm sent:
To be myself in dignity
        Free to bravely see
The price of all the effort
        Is to finally be me.

Harlequin

O Harlequin

In unmeasured grace
            and delicacy
As clever as
            the fool to see
Angelic opportunity
            to bring us
                        incongruity
            as juggling you smile on...
Haunts the vested
                        intellect
Into dreams less
                        circumspect
            a wondering
            with new respect:
                        dark intelligence
                                    is known.

Lamps

Among the lamps of morning
        Between the hills of dawn
Before the warming homefires
        We long to linger on.

As new as spring's first blossom
        This love as fresh as milk,
That steams within the morning air
        And whispers soft as silk
And stirs within the tree of life
        For hearts not young nor old
Which even for the meekest
        Inspires a passion bold.

With eyes on sleeping children
        And lips that kiss shared words
The lovers part at daybreak
        As free as winging birds.

Solstice

The hunter writes on water
        Inviting eyes to trance
With senses ringing timeless
        Captive to the dance.
So quiet by the river,
        Perched upon the stone
Haunted by a green man,
        Shouldering alone
The burden of the ages
        The glimmering of light
With ear to silent ages
        Singing in the night.
I hear the drum of evening
        I bear the flute of stars
Above us calls the singer
        Softening our scars.
Smooth away the traces
        Relieve the ancient grief
Balancing it places
        The acorn and the leaf.
Along the river walking
        Bone Woman should stand free
Within the darkness calling...
        Calling out to me.
I saw the buck was on the sand
        At dawn he stopped to drink
Nearby approached the walking doe
        Within her lifeborn link.
And in the fading sunlight
        I paused to grasp a stone
Which on a pile of others
        Appeared to me alone.

Skies

Gently wake, O slumbering heart,
Whose griefs are gone beyond my art,
And open eyes that glory knew
In nights that blazed with love for you.

Awake anew to grow with spring
To smile in brightness, and to sing
Of life undying, bright with days,
And write again the lovers' praise.

For all in all, with mate or lone,
We one day reap what is well sown.

Forever

I lift your chin to make me wise
And slowly kiss your brow and eyes
To smile into your upturned face
And share with you this human grace.

A moment of forever's call
    Encompassing a heart's last fall
A breathless gasp of clarity
   Realized, in verity.

Human

On sands between the sea and shore
               We walk as gods unknown
Our siblings fall to rise no more
               As others born are grown.

The future is a fiery storm
               The past is locked in ice
And in between our blood flows warm
               And freedom rides the dice.

But know you, and betray it not,
               When all is said and done,
Our passions are what Angels sought
               And from them Daemons run.

So beat the drums and dare to fight
               And above all fiercely love
For in the heart lives greater light
               Than in the skies above.

Image

We live within an image of
        what we think to be
And learn to question what we know
        and everything we see
And insofar as we are known
        among ourselves and clear
So far do we identify
        the people we hold dear.

Yet in my visioning the world
        and sharing what was meant
No greater mystery is near
        than messages you sent
How carefully your words I read
        in fathoming your deep
When all the while was surfacing
        the sounds of life asleep.

solo

we dreamed of merging lives in love
and dancing as close as skin,
and lingered long to draw hope of
the presence we were in.

but when our time had gone away
and distances stretched far,
then all our yearning night and day
drew near to who we are.

in emptiness between the times,
when life is shadowed grey,
the naked soul is that which rhymes
with night in every day.

so listen for your true love's call,
and wait with bated breath,
for love is that which measures all:
its loss hits deep as death.

though nothing would i seldom bring
and nothing take away:
who we are is what we sing
and what we do, the way.

Mon Malaise

Our objects name our gods,
       whose domains decide our ways
Whether wellness beats the odds
       or sad or gladness weighs.
My brood of days, wan and shallow,
       where naught and essence mix,
Are scurries after empty hopes
       Each ventured on the Styx
Like leaves of winter on a stream
       that tease my wearied gaze
As warbling waters ever flow,
       and toward that ocean laze,
In time, a span of emptiness,
       and poems incomplete,
When all the efforts to speak clear
       comingle with defeat.
As certain as that childhood wish
       to be adult and grown
So certain is the dreadful day
       when I shall die alone.
But death, O hurried dreamer,
       is but an open door,
An exit from this empty place,
       when I will write no more.

Reach

I reach to you, to touch your face,
To sense into your inner space,
Within this time our heavens lent
Our spirit song for souls silent
Rapt, with focused energies
As if in prayer on grateful knees
Our gods of life and love to please
But wake alone to dawn.

Telemachus

For harbors of the homeland watch
        Where wait our hopes and dreams
And eye on our horizon sheer
        Believing real what seems
As searching for a long-lost face
        Within the billowed cloud
While worrying that all is lost
        Though never spoke aloud:
Unending want without elation
        Yet still to watch entranced
As if invested time were banked
        Withdrawn on fulfilled chance.

Agate

Within a world of wind and stone
Where grasses sing upon the loam
       And sun and stars adore the moon
       Like children laughing in her home
So will I know you, no more alone,
And touch your hair as hearts attune
       To twinned eternal destiny
       In love's unbounded mystery.
So cast our shells aside to fly
As free as eagles, and as high,
       To see and touch our guiding star
       Two souls who living silent are
Known, in certainty at last,
Beneath the light and shadows cast
Knowing, open, fully met,
       Upon the earth, where sun has set
Beyond the sweep of ceaseless seas
       Ourselves to know,
       Ourselves to please.

Jeannette

Before the nations came to be
    And darkness gripped the land
When mercy was obscurity
    And right was strength of hand
There walked a bearer of the light
    Who taught the grim to smile
And never may I offer slight
    Till I have walked his mile.

A counselor to kings was he
    Who took his meal with thieves
Who gave his all for such as me
    As much as who believes
A man of an original mind
    Who spoke with words unsaid
Who opened eyes that once were blind
    And restored to life the dead.

Perhaps the paths into the light
    Are as many as we are
But one is known to be as right
    As sunshine to a star.

Charlene

What is within, that ever sees
among the clouds above the trees
the forms of mythos taking shape
that men would seek, and try to ape?

What source of power draws us on
when all our dreams and hopes are gone
that keeps us growing greater still
when growing is beyond our will?

Whose heart is this, within this breast,
that pulses life though death seems best
and raises eye to seek again
the glowing bloom within this fen?

Is it not the spirit's own
whose song is heard, from heaven grown?

Child

My child I raised into the night
toward the moon and bright starlight
To gaze upon the mystic lamps
       that gave our ancestry a chance
A babe of wondrous seeing eyes
       Without a mask of truths or lies
To be upheld in my young hands
My child between the skies and lands

Suit

The heft
        and balance
Of a blade:
        Honed precision.

Business

The tool of our choosing
          for our ruggedest dream
Where our golems make war
          and our parlays may seem.
As armies of levers and cold rolling wheels
          inexorably move
While our magic reveals
          the fruits of the worlds
To feed all our nations
          to shelter our lives
From darker predations
          And guiding our course
The bright star still shines
          To music born live
From the finest of minds.

Scent of Shadow

The scent of shadow lingered
   well into the dusk
In lines of knowing, waiting,
   a memory of musk

Into night to work free
   Hardly looking up
Until this sleep has swept me
   Into dream's night cup.

I dreamt there was in winter
   a widow without spring
Sweeping in her dark gowns
   dark eyes lingering,

Like a raven silent
   as silent as could be
Save only black skirts rustling
   rustling around me

And as she bent to whisper
   a meaning meant to be
I knew a sudden terror
   and struggled to get free

Yet in the waking moment
   I turn to see you gone
And gratefully can linger
   Eyes to growing dawn.

And in the day I wonder
   Wherever are you now
And under my own sunlight
   Planting where I plow,

Whatever was the knowing
    That carried you away
So grateful to have mentioned
    The night which is full day

For had you not retreated
    When I spoke names of gods
I never would have noticed
    a love against all odds.

Sun on Stone

Morning slides to wash the stone
And sunlight stretches true
Upon the rocky mountain
Beneath a wash of blue.

Where one star pins defiant
Hold firmly yet for dawn
Till sunlight grows triumphant
Beyond where hope has gone.

And on a peak of insight
Where only starlight fell
I spoke to you of moonlight
Though you were in the spell.

To dance upon the mountain
To sing with clearest voice
Drunk on daylight's fountain
Insistent on the choice...

And I can name the fool
As shadows come for me
To slip into the cool
As you wander toward the sea.

Diana

She swirled the stars falling
       In the evening of time
To live her bright calling
       Nobly sublime.

As caught up in living
       She worked to make right
A gift to be giving
       In goodness and light.

Sincerely she taught
       Of Noblesse Oblige
'Til angels have brought
       Her home to her Liege.

Theresa

I had thought to be a holy man
        One called by others wise
And fancied I might make it
        Until I met her eyes.

The depth of soul that shone there
        With light that lifts us up
The hand that gave her bread to me
        And smiled for me to sup
Has brought to us the angels
        Has brought to us a song
That David might have dreamt of
        That Solomon would long
To hear the woman laughing
        To see her living smile:
Though bent beyond all breaking
        She stood to walk His mile.

And in the stillness hear it
        And ponder in your heart
She raised our human spirit
        Beyond the reach of art.

Amethyst

You touched me
Quiet as sunlight
Warm upon the skin
Where the seawind
Had chilled
And smiled
In your eyes
Calling me
On the shore
With the waves
At our side.

And I thought
That it could happen
And I thought
It could be
for moment
shining silence
when you touched
inside of me.

But day now has fled me:
Today now has died
And I'm left
In a moment
In a dream
Of a bride.

Moliere

Awakening, eyes sang to life
           with humor free and fair
And sipped her tea in calm sunlight
           Upon her lap, Moliere.

Puzzled, I could only gaze
           and wonder of her thought
And with her smile upon my days
           I gave bouquets unbought.

In time she is no longer there
           and that life ancient ruins
Her memories to me are fair
           her words profound as runes.

Change fills our heartwings
           Celebration lifts us up.

Flaws

As if obedient to a law
When I look I have a flaw:
If I purged this soul throned heart
   of passion's urge and primal art
To rid me of the angry surge
Then among the counted loss
Would be the golden with the dross
   A husk of Man, soul bereft,
   Grey and tasteless, nothing left...
So when the storm begins to grow
I must depart: I have to go
   But darling if it's you I love
   Then, by moon and stars above,
   As sure as ebbing tides will wax
   I will return: I will be back
Though all our bridges burn aflame
I will walk them in your name
Though new walls rise and bar my way
I will besiege them, night and day
 Until the words fall from your lips
   To leave forever: Go away.
Else watch me walking whole again
Through the minefields, through the fen,
Through what labyrinths you lay...

'Til you deny me that I can
Or I can kiss you as a Man.

Emerald

A trio of birch
laid bare for winter
meet at a weathered grey stone
silent, awaiting
spring's recreating
Their emerald, whispering church:

What eyes have I to soothe their day?
what strength is called my own?
Of all the things that wisemen say
We reap what they have sown.

The stone was crowned
 with lichens and moss
Half buried in the earth
and in his shadow the seeds once fell
And wet rain gave them birth.

Beneath them in a swirling place
the light gleams dim and rare
And fragments from our history race
like leaves beyond all care.

But up against the chilling blue
their shafts are white as snow
And where their spindles touch the clouds
I heard my whistling go...

Wildflower

O gather up the wildflowers
    and race against the wind
Hold soft your love in these sweet hours
    That quickly never end
Captivate the rhapsody
    with kisses from the heart
Enchantments like that melody
    are rare enough to start.
Treasure every second tight
    each minute, every hour,
As if it might all end tonight
    and lose its tender power.

Ending the rhapsodic aire
    the music fell from me
Leaving me a silent stare
    in mute soliloquy.

Jericho

Rose the sun
        in her blood red sky
Black smoke pillars
        stung my eye
A farmer's field
        just an undug grave
A burning chapel
        where a lunatic raves
This plate of sorrows
        has turned my head
The madness came
        from among the dead...
Why am I walking?
        Where can I go?
My lady's trumpet:
        My Jericho.

Valentine

What are these seeds,
        that sprout in the dark
And grow imperceptibly
        within my world?
They crack their shells
        like hearts breaking
And reach for what is
        so far above them...
Why do they try
        as their ancestors did
So determinedly
        though doomed to fail:
Did they touch its face
        they would be blasted....
Why do they try so
        patient and quiet
So totally set on reaching
        up?
Still, I water them... as if
there were hope
as if there were
hope

Spirit

What time is left my singing soul
On earth with you who know it whole
When we might open up that world
Whence we were cast, yea, fully hurled...

Such poverty are these my words
Compared with living songs of birds
What futile tools to represent
The meanings for which they were sent...

That somehow in our final dream
We might discern them as they seem:
There is a spirit entered here
Who speaks to sound your inner ear...

Grieve for words we cannot speak
When we perceive the meaning leak
Away from what is felt to be
An impact of divinity...

What can we say to truth convey
In mortal words we throw away?
Yet word and song are coined and spent
Until the angels grow silent...

Counsel

What star rides high to guide in life
That counsels us to hide from strife?

What growth is had from burrowing deep
In a fantasy of Life asleep?

Though devastation guard the way
Pick up your staff and greet the day!
Though rubble be what's near at hand
Morticed together it builds the land.
And death awaits us, safe or not,
But alive are we now, and all unsought.

Meanwhile moments compile your years:
Never be blind, nor stop your ears,
Nor buffer your touch, nor dull your taste,
None of the senses should ever you waste.
Especially the mind, which senses our scheme,
The objects of reality, the glories of dream...

And should you discover it's all gone to hell,
Perhaps it's because no roses you smell.

Better to choose the adventurous path
Than to die at the crossroads alone with your wrath.

Silk

I adore
The lovers wrestling within
And believe there is more
Than silk seduced skin
To tempting my lover's tantalizing eyes
And reaping the fruit of her sweetest sighs
With all the night's forgotten lore
Prelude and fugue; tonal and score,
Burning an offering to gods within
Empowering the sensual magician...

In this moment I can see
Intricacies beyond my mortal me
In order for my love to be
I must release, and see her free...

But know the sensual in your mind
Seeks majesty with Womankind:
What male can more or ever hope
When all else lies beyond our scope
Than the uniting balance of making love
Which intimates divinity to this mortal glove:

Before she closes my open door
Behold the love whom I adore!

Lady

Lonely soldier of the night
Warming in the morning light
Alert to see the still unseen
Quick to slip into the green
Having lost his life before
When wife and children whom she bore
Were wrenched away in time's cruel tide
And he was left bereft of bride
And having won to his lone peak
He was a-spying there to seek
To find a solace for his age
To heal his sorrow and his rage
When low amid a shadowed vale
He saw a glass pavilion pale
Shining as a sparkling broach
A Queen could wear without reproach
And there within a crystal case
He saw a beauty beneath her face
Which shone from deep within her heart
Not placed by mortal hand nor art
Yet trapping her were ghastly specters
Shades of hellish nether vectors
Spawn of evils from the past
Within that tomb they had her cast
Fond of speculation's knack,
The soldier reached into his pack
Drew forth his shaving mirror bright
And shone the sun upon the wight
Now would you think that all is well
Before the sounding of your knell?
For all his wit and worldly rigor

He woke the lady *and* the tiger...

Twilight

Hold deep again this sinewy limb
Take heart and mind and soul within
I wait in silence as for dawn
And softly move, without moving on.
Like a dark sky's morning star
A spark in night air from afar
To invest in you the warmth I seek
So hard to find on Solace Peak.
Standing stone watch as you lay
As sure as sunrise starts the day
Listen to the meadowlark:
So you rise within my dark.
Lady, lovely in my sight
Know that I would fill your night
Though shades of whirlwinds haunt your dreams
And in the shadows work their schemes.
Brimming glass of unity
Drinking you I long to be
Casting jeweled rhythms bright
A spirit trail for your inner sight.
When night sweeps in to plunge you deep
Embracing you within your sleep
Sparking fires in body and soul
Inspiring desire's source and goal
Quickening your heart to sing
And open, like an evening rose
Soon aflame with earthy glows.

As proudly as the moon is pure
Strong and long is this allure.

Scotland

Raven eye on acorn,
         the mist swept down the vale;
The chilling blue was in the sky
         and hunger in the pale.

Her hair was red as sunset,
         her laughter good as gold,
In skin and eye was beauty kept
         That men would long to hold.

I came to her by moonlight
         a shadow on the wind
Within her warmth on that cold night
         came love without an end.

Though ages passed along the way,
         and cities rose and fell,
We seek each other day by day
         and found are as a bell.

Restless in rebirth
         we search the broadest earth.

Solace

Under the stars
Waiting, knowing nothing yet
This desert, bleak with dry wind,
Stretching away and desolate:
Deep with silence odd
Forever knowing true:
Solitude is talking to god
But Love is god talking to you.

Thunder

The wind is rising
      and the sky is black
Moist warmth blowing circles
      skittering my little campfire
The tarps crack, flown,
      Trying to cover up
Tying it down for the swelling storm, booming wet
      It's heavy and wicked, the looming threat,
A tenseness building
      into a thrill of helplessness
And now I wait facing the wind with my heart
      eyes watering
      recognizing my doom
Too late to run now
      else way to soon
Because I love every woman
like a storm shakes every window
When the thunder cracks heaven's notice
that it's damn real here
I love every woman from the tiny wall artist
To the keening willow woman
      shuddering in the winds
      I devour your wanting
      and hunger for more...

Seedling

flowing from the moist warm earth
       the seedling slips above his birth
as radiant roots beneath the soil
       draw his food to fuel his toil

sunlight warms and vibrant feeds
       leaves of green for undreamt seeds
fertile being of the day
       inspire my life and silent way

what lesson here beckons my heart?
       what thought beyond this sham of art?
oh tiny slip of growing life
       will you shade my someday wife?

Topaz

grasping silent destiny
submersed in life
      to come to be
to grow, unfold, to bloom
      to see
beyond the veiling mystery
      as if a captive of the light
yet free as ever man could be
      to stand and hold
      and laugh and love
and weep alive beneath above:
      as distant as the star to me
      yet close as breath I long to be.
the prize is in the knowing.

Ghost

It wasn't the child
Who sings in my heart
And knows the joys and sorrows of
This radiant beauty I call love
It wasn't the man
Whose form I wear
Whose calm warm hands
Adored your hair
It was rather the ghost
Whose grief and fear
Filled dreams and fictions
With jealousy's sear.
It was the ghost...
But the ghost was me
Alone in gone forever
Among the campfires of the dead
Feet in the embers
Nevermore free
We wrapped ourselves in each other's dream
Hoping to reach the real from the seem
Entwining our mingling aspiration
Then worried about the strange elation.
Meaningless dances with empty eyes
Conditioned responses, insincere sighs,
Conspire to make the weariest hope
The ghosts of the other will allow us to cope.
The ghastly masks we swap and trade
Seem all too real to keep what's made.
There came a moment in the unmade bed
Haunted with pillows for no one's head
When all had been said, and decision's ride
Came to the Bridge of Groom and Bride.
Whatever the choice results from romance
Beware my friend, of the Old Ghost Dance.

Hill

Uncommon rush, to so hear my name,
Spoken melodious, a rare gift it came.
The question before me is whether to bear
A singing young woman of scented red hair
And forego the echoing psalter of choice
Purely in pleasure of hearing her voice.
Well, perhaps a bit more, but pleasant be still
If I would but make of this mountain a hill.
The mountain is heavy: I carried it here
It's made of the ash of a very deaf ear.
If I would then make of this mountain a hill
Then she would go with me, methinks that she will.
If she would go with me then perish the day
When mountainous hills will not go away.
If mountainous hills will not go away
Their faith is the greater, and I could not stay.
But if she went with me what matters it yet
Whether hills go away, or we away get?
The hills are away lass; the hills are away!
So come to me darlin', we'll live for the day!
Come to me sweetheart and sweep up the stars
The passions of romance are most truly ours.

Husk

Frames of reference cast away
the contexts of our yesterday
leaving just the husks of seeds
that mark the consequence of deeds
the nourishment on which we fed
to nurture life for what we said
is sown into our histories
and mutates from those mysteries.
someday a harvest will we reap
to feed the undreamt dreams asleep
which here and now begin to grow
like acorns deep beneath a snow.
people cast away the frame
when solving naught and fixing blame:
best capture all the crucible's dross
than lose the golden with the toss.
yet if it matters not to you
whether growth should have value
ephemera you have and hold
unexpectant of the old.
since in your mortal tent you dwell
so briefly time you cannot tell
to walk within and be without
breeds eloquence in the devout.

Dilemma

Choosing the loss of one or both
When what matters most is on the oath
Is hellish, for a tender man:
To lose it all? Or lose again?
Life is too short to waste the breath
When even our values define our death:
Life's virtue better defines the man
Thus what he sought was in his hand.
Yet here I stand at this crossroads
Far from the din of the chains and goads
To choose my path within this wood
Unable to tell between evil and good.
On the one hand I stand to lose my love
On the other I lose the stars above
This way all is tangled and sharp,
But that way deafens away the harp.
I could decide to let it go
And let the waters call the throw
Or yet again I could play it smart
And lose the soul within my heart...
Perhaps I should just stand right here
And choose to not choose, out of fear
And then the Fates would take control
And all I'd lose would be my goal...
But then what if I just began
To turn around, and then I ran
Far back along the way I've come
But oh... to what an erring sum!
It's at these times when brilliant men
Begin to wonder, and again...

Ocean

The waves throw back my longing
The gulls decry my thoughts
But walking in the salt wind
A stillness smooths my knots.

Within the ocean's knowing
Within the sea's own mind
I sense a song of changing
And curious, I find
The choices are quite near
In every waking step
That on my way I'm taking
A treasure I have kept.

And as I turn to landward
Where someday she will rise
Behind me waits an ocean
A truth before me lies.

Fall

Warm as autumn rivers
        bearing golden leaves
Another year is turning
        turning with the breeze
And we will not replace it
        cycled out of mind
Nor can we quite grasp it
        washing away time
As in a forest golden
        where leaves unbidden fall
We worry for a profit
        though all we have is all.

Laura

O, Laura,
That ever night would win
A consequence of dreaming
        And where I long have been
To walk among the wildflowers
        Where sunlight once had shone
To give to you at morning
        Wet with dew alone.
What meanings beckon
        Out of dream,
That hope would rise
        From the unseen
Already, as if there were more
        Than has been yet,
Yet stands the door impossibly open.
I should have studied harder then
I should have learned by now, my friend,
Yet here am I already there
As if in hope I had no care
        As if the night had never known
        As if my life were never thrown
        By anguished fear and rage, unfair
        At all the crushing sadness there
        That ripped aside my roof and wall
        And flung me down to grieving thrall
        Bereft of spark or laugh or smile
        Cleft from dream and offered bile
Left beside the road for dead
Without a stone to rest my head
Until, for lack of else to do,
I once more stand
        Awake to you.

You gifted a quiet smile.

Friend

A friend of fine appointment
            confided loss and fear
A mother with her children
            Well and growing near
With seven bonny darlings
            afforded all she had
Recovering from a nightmare
            that took away their Dad
And I must pause in wondering.

Here is a test of values
            issuing from the day
That in the darkness slumbers
            and struggles into gray:

Is mine an honest friendship?

Water

Beneath the whispering alder leaves
    Children play, and no one grieves
Laughter spikes the woodland air
    children smile and grownups care.
Sheltered in the world above
    tender couples mingle love
Passion wanes, passion waxes
    inviting closer human access,
First of touch, a first embrace
    first caressing of the face
        Loving grip of emotional heat
        Sweeps away cool reason's seat.
           Cresting swell of oceanic life
        Lift the linked above vain strife
        Surging higher, engulfing all
        Beyond where lovers still could fall
        Beyond the reach of time and space
        To that plateau where glows the face
           Of gods in glory, laughing...

All becalm withdrawn release
    The drawing back, the kiss of peace,
The hollowness, the vacancy
    The loss of true reality...
        Yet those who love are gathered still
        Touching yet, kisses fulfill
           Aspiring that love might linger on
           As if the night would bring no dawn
           Weaving a desirous chord
        He, his lady; She, her lord,
        ...and on into the fire's coals
        a promise kept where are no goals.

Every Night, tonight.

Sparks

Windswept sparks whip brightly aside
    the scudding campfires try to hide
Down low among the fieldstone ring
    from the wind, whose impatient moans
Crack the branches of night
    and still I stand watch... waiting...

Somewhere far away tonight
    a woman sleeps by candlelight
Of whom she dreams I cannot see
    but I see her clearly, in front of me...

As I stand and count the stars
    and await the desperate call of Mars
Her scent I smell, her skin I feel
    although a dream as much as real
I see someday her smile for me
    and ache inside that I were free
To walk now all that hopeful road
    and hold her in the wordless ode.

The Fool

I know it isn't wise
    to open up that door
To walk out in your moonlight
    as I have done before...
I know it isn't sensible
    to bet it all again
When passion makes me vulnerable
    and odds don't think I'll win...
There is but one affirming thing
    that keeps me moving on
And that's how happily I rise
    to greet the morning's dawn.

Lay your precious head across
    my chest again tonight
and tell me that you love me
    and that everything's alright.

Some things are soon forgotten
    and some things never die
I've dreamed of you so often
    in daylight's alibi
The danger seems an old friend
    as innocent as a smile:
Though angels try to mend this heart
    they fear to walk my mile.

But lay your head across me
    and comfort me with lies
I'll fall for your known fallacies
    and think the foolish wise.

Flores por los Muertos

After the glow and fire are known
    and the hot attraction is outworn
The new body has been explored, skin to bone,
    then rise old ghosts, new reborn:
Flores! Flores por los Muertos!

Flowing out of odd dark corners
    In husks of memory
Sculpting time strips love to scorn
    Ground with anguished emory:
Flores! Flores por los Muertos!

Suggesting, reminding, come what may,
    Whatever we do is like yesterday
In crucial moments suppose and replace
    slipping the death mask on a living face:
Flores! Flores por los Muertos!

Like ravening vampires undismayed
    They draw the life from love displayed
Trying to jealously doom happiness
    Of the new bloom they suck holiness:
Flores! Flores por los Muertos!

Beware, then, O lovers, and fashion
    after love is undeniably said
Between your talk and throes of passion
    offer flowers for your dead:
Flores! Flores por los Muertos!

Lost Issue

As time revolves around an age
        And elders wonder true
The young to life would seek a sage
        And solve the lost issue.

And in our mantled visioning
        Encrusted with our years
The important we are pondering
        While youth dies at our ears.

All the wildest quests abuse,
        That sparked our kindled minds,
Still we dismiss as ancient news
        What the quickened finds.

Oh, they will learn that questions age
        As surely as did we
But we, as ours, still fail to gauge
        The currents of life's sea.

Mist

Having seen the pleasant days
When mists, diffused with golden rays,
Carried here your garden scent
And dampened vine with dew
An ancient heart is startled
With eyes awake for you.

Quiet fingers trim the vine
And test the leaves with care
The swelling grapes are sweetening
As morning clears the air
Again a sound of quickening
With eyes in quest for you.

Then in, to lonely breakfasting
And coffee on the porch
Chill morning warming slowly, shines
And sipping sweetened steaming cup
I close my eyes in quest for you.

Waking

At the moment of our waking
        From what we thought would be
While time swells like a storm front
        Looming out to sea
I ask of you the question
        Of what you wish to know
And answering you ask me
        Where do the children go?

And here upon this headland
        Where paths away divide
Where often blowing beach sand
        Will our footprints hide
We pause to know the beauty
        Like as the sweeping sea
And answering must hold you
        Tenderly to me.

Laura's Sonnet

When snap of chill invites the green to gold
And hearth in warmth and light makes welcome
home
Then magnified are details left untold
In spring a quip, in harvest heavy tome.

And grown alike as children from their toys
When falls away the need to each possess
We give our moments as our daily joys
And build the tales within our lives' caress.

Companionship in comfort, aged in love,
Our hurried work of building for the night
Our young adventure filled to stars above
This life to our potential's full requite.

Our moment of forever yet to fill
Our moment of shared dreaming beckons still.

Moment

We dance within the framework of our lives
Advancing evolution in our minds
Averring that the seeker sometimes finds
No matter how benightedly he strives.

So reach across the threshold of your time
And yearn for what you doubt may ever stay
Embraced by haunting memories gone away
Wearing your tomorrows for their rhyme.

And as for my beloved and her me
The moment stands eternal in the glow
Cherishing the present that we know
In passionate betrothal like a sea.

To celebrate the being of this love
Now freed of shackling culture's legacy
Two lives like living lamps of prophecy
That cause the dance our hearts are beating of.

So in the mortal sense of this embrace
Before uncertain fires of what will be
And after that which was has gone from me:
In tenderness this light adores your face.

Fear

Whatever falls upon this unfilled time
That creeps upon my page like shadow's fall
And captures up the errant twisting rhyme
To wrest from me the perfect lover's call?

What fear within me wrestles passion's dance
And sings to me the griefs of past love's fall
Yet grasping firm, believing in the chance
That faith in your revealing may save all?

So waiting for deliverance in these hours
While worried that unease has found his bride
To steal away the treasure that was ours
 And take my place to lead you from my side.

One mention of discomfort I received
Yet all my world awaits a word believed.

Release

And then upon the further page
Where dragons burn and daemons rage
Against the rising of the sun
The freedom to be me stands clear
As bells of gladness din the ear
And opens up the eyes of one
Who named the hellspawn in his age
Releasing freedom from her cage.

And on release and claiming free
The fear hath fled away from me
For she within her own light knows
The rage against eternal night
Where I must wage my spirit's fight
For wellness within our love grows
Despite this errant wandering
As I await at passion's spring.

Ritual

Ritual springs from my lady's sweet dance
Golden hair soft as the breeze, to my glance,
Rising to kiss from the midst of her day,
Deftly caressing my troubles away.

In the cool evening I find my way home
Scent the good cooking and lift up the tome
She has left open to personal choice
Gifting a passage that speaks in her voice.

Bells from a garden may call us to dine;
Golden of Autumn may sweeten sunshine:
Such is my sensing of my lady's eye
On my soul sleeping when morning is nigh.

When upon waking I stroke her soft cheek,
Whisper her name like the rhyme that I seek,
Then, like a rhapsody's unbroken aire,
Gladness awakens, with both of us there.

Chance

From the sad day I was first disappointed
      From a fond childhood of well-schooled
illusion
From grim day benighted, so aptly appointed
      With brooding despair and wildest
confusion,
This woman awakens me to laughter and joy
      I have not felt since I was a small boy.

Now the moment of which all poets sang
      That balances books to this spiritual
wealth
With redeeming happiness' savory tang
      A gift as from heaven in surfeit of health
That evil black dragons of grief are as slain
      When this woman's sunlight
           broke through my sad rain

Tangle

Within a past of winding ways
       Oft where anguish lay in wait
In darkness tangled up with greys
       And sunlight glinting rare and great
Within the thorned and twisted wild
       Grown from earthen mother's child,
I sought my rest from grief profound
       From mystery, from harrowed plight,
And to myself my heart I bound
       While loping toward a hopeful light
Mentioned in the ancient words
       And hinted in the flight of birds.

Still now upon this golden plain
       Where often sunlight dwells of late
Where grasses green with gentle rain
       And night of stars will populate
The dome above this freedom hold
       As young as life, and as old,
I find a solace in her ways
       A meal to eat and bed to warm
A merry meeting for my days
       And speak my mind, an' it no harm,
Writing my unbidden words
       Of winged hearts that soar as birds.

Jade Temple

As in a garden, dreaming,
        I heard a distant bell
Cast in ancient meaning
        A future to foretell
Amid the bones of spirit
        Amid the clattered signs
Surrounded by strange context
        Where angled are the lines
I note my needs in silence
        Among the songs of birds
And wait the hand of justice
        To clarify my words:
Accept the precious unknown.

www.ingramcontent.com/pod-product-compliance
Lightning Source LLC
LaVergne TN
LVHW051658080426
835511LV00017B/2628